YOUR KNOWLEDGE HA

Bibliographic information published by the German National Library:

The German National Library lists this publication in the National Bibliography; detailed bibliographic data are available on the Internet at http://dnb.dnb.de .

Imprint:

Copyright © 2018 GRIN Verlag
Print and binding: Books on Demand GmbH, Norderstedt Germany
ISBN: 9783668772083

This book at GRIN:

https://www.grin.com/document/433231

Melanie Hahn

Impact of Social Media on Strengthening Brand Loyalty in the Austrian Wine Industry

GRIN Verlag

GRIN - Your knowledge has value

Since its foundation in 1998, GRIN has specialized in publishing academic texts by students, college teachers and other academics as e-book and printed book. The website www.grin.com is an ideal platform for presenting term papers, final papers, scientific essays, dissertations and specialist books.

Visit us on the internet:

http://www.grin.com/

http://www.facebook.com/grincom

http://www.twitter.com/grin_com

IMPACT OF SOCIAL MEDIA ON STRENGTHENING BRAND LOYALTY IN THE AUSTRIAN WINE INDUSTRY

BACHELOR PAPER I

submitted at the
IMC Fachhochschule Krems
(University of Applied Sciences)

Bachelor programme
International Wine Business

by
Melanie HAHN
for the award of the academic degree
Bachelor of Arts in Business (BA)

Submitted on: 15.06.2018

Table of Contents

1 Introduction

In past couple of years, social media has shaped the way of communication between brands and consumers and has opened the door for more interactive, personalized and engaging marketing strategies to increase not only brand awareness but also to build stronger customer-brand relationships that lead to brand loyalty (Yoshida, Gordon, Nakazawa, Shibuya, & Fujiwara, 2018, p. 208; Muntinga, Moorman, & Smit, 2011, p. 34-36).

There is a lot of literature on engagement in brand-related online content and social media. Yoshida et al. (2018, p.216) define brand-related social media engagement as a voluntary contribution of an individual to the interaction between her/his favourite brand and other fellow brand users by sharing information, activating and co-creating content related to the specific brand. A customer's voluntary contribution that is brand and/or product related is known as consumer engagement (Verhoef, Reinartz, & Krafft, 2010, p. 247)

Wine is often consumed within a social gathering. The product can be easily approached by engaging intuitive senses like the sense of taste and sense of smell. Therefore, it is a product to effortlessly strike up a conversation, get emotionally involved with, and exchange impressions within a social group. Consumers are very likely to have an opinion about the wine they tasted and are often enthusiastic to share it. This makes a wine-related brand seem predestined to gain from social media and might create new beneficial opportunities in the wine industry (Szolnoki et al., 2014b, p. 81). Social media enables brands to communicate on more layers and give the customer insights into the business' history, philosophy and values in combination with descriptive information about the product/brand itself (Dolan & Goodman, 2017, p. 24). Interactive environments on social networking sites enable a two-way communication between consumers and brands which has a positive impact on the brand relationship, trust and also brand loyalty (Enginkaya & Yilmaz, 2014, p. 220).

The paper is structured the following way. The first section (the research question) gives more detail on the topic and identified research gaps in the literature. The methodology summarizes the specific ways research has been concluded for this paper. The focal point lies on the literature review and analysis of several case studies and findings. It summarizes and combines two main research topics, brand loyalty on social media and social media utilization in the (Austrian) wine industry. This literature review contributes to further research about specific impacts of social media on the wine industry. In this case with a focus on Austrian wine producers. Furthermore, this BA1 includes a table of content and a rough project plan for the proposed BA II.

2 Research Question

Research Question: Does the utilization of social media by Austrian wine producers has an impact on strengthening the consumer-brand loyalty?

The aim of this research paper is to determine the influence social media has on strengthening brand loyalty and if this also applies to the Austrian wine industry. There has been a lot of research done on social media in general, specific social media networking sites and marketing strategies that show an impact on a customer's loyalty to brands they interact and engage with on social media (on a regular basis). This paper analyses different strategies on social media that have shown to deepen brand loyalty as well as examines what brand loyalty actually is, what impact brand loyalty has on a customer's purchasing behaviour and how it might benefit a brand/business to reach a new set of potential customers.

Social media has been used as a marketing tool in almost any industry including businesses and organisations revolving around the product wine. Although there is a lot of research published regarding the topics mentioned above, many papers focus on different industries or specific data of certain countries and regions. Little to no research focuses on Austrian businesses. A research gap can also be found within the Austrian wine industry. No literature examines the influence of social media utilized by wineries or wine regions in Austria.

Research conducted about other worldwide (wine) businesses or regions lay the groundwork for this paper. Case studies and findings about how social media influences brand loyalty in Australia, the USA, France, Italy or Germany sets a basis to develop hypothesis that might also apply for Austria. Especially data from Germany could give insights into how the utilization of social media in the Austrian wine industry influences brand loyalty, as these two countries share many cultural qualities and characteristics. Still, Austria is a different country and it is necessary to conduct research to draw final conclusions. Furthermore, it is essential to determine if social media strategies applied by other countries are relevant for the Austrian wine industry, if they need to be adapted and to clarify (if needed) the required adaption in detail.

3 Methodology

The research for this paper was conducted over a time period of 4 months and comprises a literature review. The main focus was set to find research papers that elaborate the influence of social media on brand loyalty in the wine industry. Keywords such as social media, brand loyalty, wine, social media engagement, social media communication, digital communication, wine industry, brand identity, social media community, consumer engagement, Austria, Austrian wine and various combinations of these keywords were used for the search in online databases. These databases include Science Direct, Emerald and Business Source Complete and were accessed from the IMC Krems Libary. All these databases set the focus on business-related research and therefore cover the main topic of this paper – marketing and more in-depth social media.

In addition to searching for keywords, the time frame for the search included only papers that were published in the last 2 years (2016-2018). This is important to mention because social media, its networking platforms and features are evolving and changing in a fast pace and research that has been conducted 5 years ago might already be outdated and not relevant anymore.

The search of the above-mentioned keywords was also conducted in specific journals to find even more relevant and valuable literature. Among those journals were the Journal of Interactive Marketing, the International Journal of Wine Marketing, the International Journal of Wine Research and the Journal of Business Research.

References within certain papers were other starting points to the research that has been gone into writing this paper. Most definitions and more general background came from papers which were referenced by recently published ones. The databases or Google Scholar provided the access to these referenced research papers or books.

A brief review of the most relevant literature can be found in the annex (Table 1: Brief Literature Review).

4 Literature Review & Analysis

A relevant literature review and analysis is fundamental to approach an academic project. It is the foundation for future research projects to build upon developed theories and findings. Furthermore, an effective analysis of scientific literature uncovers areas where there is a lack of previous research (Webster & Watson, 2002, p. xiii). This literature examines the growing impact of social media, how wine brands utilize social networking platforms (worldwide and in Austria) and which effects social media might have on brand loyalty. Elements such as brand trust and engagement on social media are in close relation to brand loyalty and therefore are also considered and investigated for this literature review.

4.1 Social Media and Its Growing Impact

Social media has changed the way businesses operate, organizational communication and public relations. Organizations utilize the easy accessibility and the possibility to reach and interact with a large crowd and helps to understand the needs of consumers (Brogan, 2010; Tajudeen, Jaafar, & Ainin, 2018, p. 308). Social Media might be best described as a group of Internet-based applications such as mobile apps or online communities. It enables users to create, share and engage with content (Kaplan & Haenlein, 2010, p. 62). These platforms enable direct consumer-brand interactions (Osei-Frimpong & McLean, 2018, p. 12). Its rapid growth has been pushed by the availability of mobile portable devices and the introduction of 3G internet surfing speed. (Alarcón, Sepúlveda, Valenzuela-Fernández, & Gil-Lafuente, 2018, p. 104) The most popular forms of social media are blogs and microblogs, Social/Business Networks like Facebook or LinkedIn or Media-Sharing Sites such as Instagram or YouTube (Alarcón et al., 2018, p. 104; Saravanakumar & SuganthaLakshmi, 2012, p. 4444).

Findings of Alarcón et al. (2018, p. 107) show that social media has the capability to influence a consumer's purchasing behaviour. To enable the beneficial interactive communication between consumers and organizations and consumers, businesses started to integrate social networking features into their websites. These features also reinforced the site's credibility to visitors. Also because of its ability to reach a mass audience at minimal cost and time, organizations and businesses expand to social media platforms and add or partially replace their traditional marketing strategies with communicating and engaging with customers online (Tajudeen et al., 2018, p. 315). The low-cost aspect, the power of customization and uncomplicated handling of these platforms increase the relevancy for not only large firms but also for small and medium-sized companies and sole proprietors (Enginkaya & Yilmaz, 2014, p. 220; Tajudeen et al., 2018, p. 314)

4.1.1 Brands on Social Media

The development of social media platforms such as Facebook, Instagram or YouTube brought a new form of brand-consumer interaction with it. Brands are able to create their own channel/profile which then can be followed by other users of the individual platform (Breitsohl, Kunz, & Dowell, 2015, p. 1042). Social media profiles personify a brand. This brand profile interacts with other profiles in the same way as friends or other human participants would. They use the same level and pattern of communication and therefore consumers can relate and react to the brand as if they were talking to a person (Barcelos, Dantas, & Sénécal, 2018, p. 67). It is important to create a sense of community and a connection between the consumer and the brand (Enginkaya & Yilmaz, 2014; p. 220). This online environment serves firms in the same way as other marketing approaches. Businesses use it to maintain and establish profitable and lasting customer relationships. Brand-hosted media profiles make it possible to provide product information, special offers, customer service and share a brand's philosophy and culture in various ways (Breitsohl et al., 2015, p. 1047). Still, different platforms require different approaches to achieve a strengthened customer loyalty (Coelho, Rita, & Santos, 2018, p. 104).

The findings of Nisar & Whitehead (2016, p. 747) list the most popular reasons why individuals follow brand pages on social networking sites. Among them are: obtaining general information about new products, read reviews and product rankings and follow the latest events and happenings related to the specific brand. Social media provides a two-way communication between a brand and the public (Simon & Tossan, 2018, p.181; Tajudeen et al., 2018, p. 314). This makes it easier to innovate and adapt strategies to improve the relationship with current followers and enhance the attractiveness of the brand's profile to potential new consumers (Tajudeen et al., 2018, p.314). It is not only a two-way communication between a customer and the brand but also a conversation between two or more customers about the brand. This allows users to better understand the brand's public relations and communication practices (Simon et al., 2018, p. 181).

4.1.2 Social Media in Austria

Social media is defined as either a social network, multimedia content sharing websites, blog or microblog. Only very little is known about the implementation of social media Austrian households and businesses. In 2013, 39% of the enterprises registered in Austria used some sort of social media. Four years later, in 2017, it was already 53% (Statistics Austria, 2017). Therefore, this explicit percentage increase in Austria reflects international statistics and support numerous findings, that the use of social media is becoming increasingly important.

Among the various social media platform, Facebook appears to be the most popular one in Austria but also in Germany and Switzerland (Martin, 2017, p. 265). The results of a cross-cultural study by (Makri & Schlegelmilch, 2017) also found out that Austrian are more likely to engage on social networking sites in comparison to Chinese or citizens of Uruguay.

The statistics of the year 2017 present the following data: The presence on social media increases with the size of an enterprise. Only 51% of small enterprises, 61% of medium-sized and already 75% of large enterprises utilize social media in some way (Statistics Austria, 2017). According to Szolnoki et al. (2014a, p. 5) about 44% of the wineries use social media to communicate with customers. Facebook is seen as the most important platform followed by Youtube, Twitter and Google Plus. Social media is already an important marketing tool in Austria and the majority of businesses plan to extend their online activity.

4.2 Social Media Engagement

Social media engagement indicates actions of individuals on brand-related posts. Sharing, liking, contributing and commenting, advocating and co-creating are essential for social media engagement and reflect an individual's willingness to interact with a brand (Muntinga et al., 2011, p. 17; Leek, Canning, & Houghton, 2016, p. 25). The popularity of a brand relates to the number of likes, comments and shares of the brand's content, therefore, is an important metric for businesses to measure brand engagement and prestige (Swani, Milne, Brown, George Assaf, & Donthu, 2017, p. 83).

To stimulate engagement a business should aim to create a psychological identification between the brand and the user/consumer. This can be achieved by satisfying the needs for entertainment (e.g value of reading, watching videos, seeing photos) before implementing sales promotions and purchase incentives. People tend to share positive, funny and extraordinary things online. Most users renounce to share sad or tragic events. Entertainment in all forms plays a fundamental role and converges on social media platforms (Erdogomus & Cicek, 2012, p. 1359). The entertainment value of a brand is related to brand loyalty (Yoshida et al., 2018, p. 216).

Enginkaya & Yilmaz (2014, p. 222) name five distinct motivations of consumers to engage with brand-related content: brand affiliation, conversation, opportunity seeking, entertainment and investigation. The content on various platforms should aim to be firm generated and to represent the businesses standards, philosophy and culture (Osei-Frimpong et al., 2018, p. 16). Findings of Simon et al. (2018, p.181) point out that reading and engaging with a brand's post as well as actively supporting a brand is part reciprocal responses of grateful consumers. Marketers attempt to target these customers in order to reach their network of friends and associates (Leek et al., 2016, p. 27).

4.2.1 Effects of Social Media Engagement

Engagement of users on social media platforms has several positive effects for brands and businesses. Interactions with brand-related content display to currently not engaged users the nature of communication and relationship a brand aims to establish with its brand community/followers and customers (Simon et al., 2018, p. 181). Engagement also illustrates a consumer's continuous brand loyalty intention (Hollebeek, Glynn, & Brodie, 2014, p. 150). It is indispensable for managers to neglect the numbers of engagement (Habibi, Laroche, & Richard, 2014, p. 159). Users not only engage with content and brands they are following but furthermore see content which is popular among their friends, very similar to word-of-mouth recommendations in everyday life (Erdogomus & Cicek, 2012, p. 1359).

Social media closely resembles a digital ("new") word-of-mouth (WoM) effect also referred to as e-WoM (Enginkaya & Yilmaz, 2014, p. 220; Osei-Frimpong et al., 2018, p. 16). It integrates a user's own voice and reaches his/her following and friends (Enginkaya & Yilmaz, 2014, p. 220). Findings of Osei-Frimpong et al. (2018, p. 18) advise firms to actively engage followers and potential customers on social media to enhance the brand-relationship and loyalty intentions (Dwivedi, 2015, p. 107). Both lead to a positive impact on e-WoM (Osei-Frimpong et al., 2018, p. 16) and consumers are more likely to buy products and services of brands they have been following and engaging with on social media platform (Nisar et al., 2016, p. 748).

4.2.2 Social Media Community: Engagement & Trust

Brand communities, in general, can be defined as virtual or physical places for people to connect and socialize with and about a specific brand they admire (McAlexander, Schouten, & Koenig , 2002, p. 44). Online networking sites are the ideal environment to build brand communities (Habibi et al., 2014, p. 159). Habibi et al. (2014, p. 159) furthermore, identified four essential relationships to build a brand community: customer-product, customer-brand, customer-company and customer-other customer. Many important tasks are performed in brand communities like other members of the community can step into the function of the support service department to reply to questions and concerns by describing personal experiences with the brand/product (Schau, Muñiz, & Arnould, 2009, p. 40, Habibi et al., 2014, p. 159). Such interactions also make the brand appear to be more trustworthy in the eyes of consumers (Habibi et al., 2014, p. 153).

Brand community identification and engagement has a positive effect on the brand relationship and subsequently has a beneficial effect on brand loyalty, purchase intentions (Algesheimer, Dholakia, & Herrmann, 2005, p. 33) and brand trust (Casaló, Flavián, & Guinalíu, 2007; Habibi et al., 2014, p. 153). Recent findings of (Yoshida et al., 2018, p. 216) underline these effects but argue that engagement on social media contributes more to brand loyalty than online community identification does. Online brand communities implement a more personal distribution of content and the convenience to reach a broader audience of prospective customers (Enginkaya & Yilmaz, 2014, p. 220).

4.3 Social Media Impact on Brand Loyalty

The basic structure of social media platforms is to enable highly interconnected networks of people (customers) making it uncomplicated to share information in a short amount of time (Chu & Kim, 2011, p. 47). The networks all share the characterisitics of a sense of community, openness and being connected and able to communicate with others. These characteristics create an ideal environment for brands seeking to engage with consumers and initiate brand loyalty (Enginkaya & Yilmaz, 2014, p. 220). Research by Tajudeen et al. (2018, p. 315) ascertained that businesses utilizing social media marketing effectively simultaneously to offline marketing campaigns are able to improve the brand relationship and increase the loyalty of customers. Beyond that, the understanding of achieving brand loyalty improves sales revenues, profitability to the business (Keller , Parameswaran, & Jacob, 2011) improved perception of the product performance, additional business extension opportunities, marketing success and the competitive advantage (Dolan & Goodman, 2017, p. 28).

Laroche, Habibi, & Richard (2013, p. 78) found out that participation in virtual communities positively influences customer-brand relationships and enhances trust. Their research additionally identifies brand trust as a key prerequisite to achieving loyalty. Marketers are certain that brand loyalty amplifies by creating a closer connection with consumers online as well as offline (Coelho et al., 2018, p. 109). Maintaining consumer relationships relies more an more on creating value and no longer on providing better products and services (Nisar et al., 2016, p. 751). Effective two-way communication between the brand and consumers, sharing information and interacting with other community members add to the value of a brand on social media (Laroche et al., 2013, p. 80).

4.4 Social Media Utilization in the Wine Industry

Within the global wine industry, different approaches to the utilization of social media can be identified. "New World" wine producing countries have a stronger presence on social networking sites than the traditional wine producing countries in Europe (Galati, Crescimanno, Tinervia, & Fagnani, 2017, p. 41). About 87% of Australian wineries (Szolnoki et al., 2014a, p. 9) and 94% of US wineries use Facebook whereas only 60% of German (Szolnoki et al., 2014b, p. 86) and 53% of French wineries are present on Facebook (Galati et al., 2017, p. 41). The cross-cultural study by Szolnoki et al. (2014a, p. 9) analysing the social media usage within the wine business, reveals that social media was ranked the third most common way for Australian wineries to communicate with consumers. Key intentions are to attract new customers, communicate with the customers, achieve advertising for the winery, public relations and to provide information about events. Facebook also was the most popular platform for German wineries followed by Youtube and blogs (Szolnoki et al., 2014b, p. 87).

High levels of competition among small and medium-sized wine producers lead companies to seek out new and innovative marketing and communication strategies (Dolan & Goodman, 2017, p. 28). Wineries benefit from the social networking abilities of online platforms due to the possibility of consumers to spread their opinions, exchange information about the product and encourage others to try different wines (Galati et al., 2017, 42). Consumers feel more comfortable to recommend wines to others, after reading reviews on the brand's profile page. Furthermore, the number and quality of reviews add weight to a consumer's perception of quality. Brands on social media are perceived as more modern, interested in recent/ongoing happenings and with a genuine aim to interact with their consumers to build a relationship and not only make money out of their customers.

Lots of wineries use social media to give more insights into the philosophy and family history or to showcase the region and local events (Dolan & Goodman, 2017, p. 28).

4.5 Content Strategies of Wineries on Social Media

(Dolan & Goodman, 2017, p. 26ff) classify the communication approach of wineries on social media into three categories: selling orientation, customer orientation & experimental orientation.

- **Selling orientation**: focuses on sales and promotion of the brand and its available products; frequent elements within social media posts are price, release date and availability mentions of wines, tasting notes and the words like "sale", "promotion" or "new release". Photos often display medals and awards or scanned wine reviews.

- **Customer orientation**: aims to build a sense of community, trust and personal relationships with the consumer; this approach grants consumers insights into the daily happenings and activities at the winery. Everything from photos of the winery employees, information about the family and the wine processing to humorous photos of winery pets and cartoons. It does not include information about prices or promotional images of the wine region.

- **Experimental orientation**: promotes specific experiences offered by the winery such as events or wine tastings; usually the photos capture moments at events organized by the winery or that take place in the winery like weddings and musical performances, The photos also showcase the event facilities and the preparations for events. Often mentioned are the date, ticket price and how to book the venue.

The classification of content and what it depicts is as important for engagement as the regular continuity of sharing content on social media (Simon et al., 2018, p. 182). Campaigns should be entertaining, fun and at the same time informative (Erdogomus & Cicek, 2012, p. 1359). The use of images, short videos and creative messages arouse the interest of consumers to interact with the winery and therefore enhance the loyalty (Osei-Frimpong et al., 2018, p. 18) Photos showcasing the local landscape, the cellar door, experiences at the winery, the staff and family, help consumer to get a better understanding of the business. The brand feels more familiar which influences the purchasing behaviour and enhances brand trust. Consumers are more likely to buy wines (Dolan & Goodman, 2017, 29). Frequent updates several times a week and answering customers quickly reinforces brand intimacy and encourages people to follow the brand's profile (Simon et al., 2018, p. 181).

5 Conclusion & Further Research

Social media has become a relevant approach for businesses to communicate and interact with their (prospective) consumers. Continuous engagement with brands online enhances the brand-consumer relationship. This relationship also based on brand trust which ultimately results in improving the loyalty of consumer to a specific brand and furthermore the purchasing behaviour. Wine businesses worldwide are present on social networking sites. For small and medium-sized wine producers it offers the great possibility to communicate with large amounts of consumers on a personal level while still having relatively low costs in comparison to marketing campaigns with similar outcomes. A large percentage of wine producers in the "New World" countries like the USA or Australia already incorporated Social Media into their marketing strategies. In most European countries and especially in Austria only about half (or a little over half) of the wine producers utilize social networking sites thus far and many more plan to extend their online presence to social media in the near future.

The specific effects of social media on brand loyalty are broadly researched among many industries. Still, there is little to no research that applies this general research for the wine industry and examines the effects for wine producers. Content on wine brand pages can be classified according to the main orientation of the business. It can be a customer orientation, experience orientation or selling orientation. Further research on the impacts of social media on brand loyalty for wine producers can be conducted by taking these three content classifications as the basic key elements. Studies can investigate the distinct impacts of each category on brand loyalty to propose the most effective content strategy on social media for Austrian wine producers if they want to improve brand loyalty. Future studies may focus for example on the combination of categories, on a certain generation (millennials, generation x, baby boomers,...) or a specific target group like consumers of different countries (Austria, USA, Japan, China, ...) which is of interest when the winery has specified wine markets they sell their wines to.

6 Table of Content BA II

This is a proposed table of contents for the BA II to get an overview of the potential structure.

Statutory Declaration

Abstract

Table of contents

7 Timetable / Project Plan BA II

The timetable illustrated the proposed processes to finalise the BA II paper. The steps are structured in a timeline and the individual steps are associated and should be accomplished in the proposed months/ time frame.

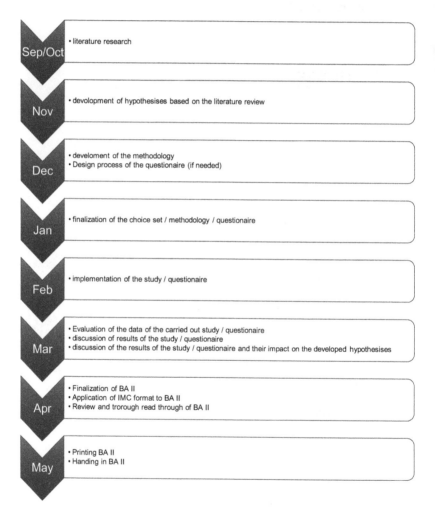

Sep/Oct
- literature research

Nov
- devolopment of hypothesises based on the literature review

Dec
- develoment of the methodology
- Design process of the questionaire (if needed)

Jan
- finalization of the choice set / methodology / questionaire

Feb
- implementation of the study / questionaire

Mar
- Evaluation of the data of the carried out study / questionaire
- discussion of results of the study / questionaire
- discussion of the results of the study / questionaire and their impact on the developed hypothesises

Apr
- Finalization of BA II
- Application of IMC format to BA II
- Review and trorough read through of BA II

May
- Printing BA II
- Handing in BA II

8 Bibliography

Alarcón, C. N., Sepúlveda, A. U., Valenzuela-Fernández, L., & Gil-Lafuente, J. (2018). Systematic mapping on social media and its relation to business. *European Research on Management and Business Economics, 24*(2), 104-113.

Algesheimer, R., Dholakia, U., & Herrmann, A. (July 2005). The Social Influence of Brand Community: Evidence from European Car Clubs. *Journal of Marketing, 69*(3), 19-34.

Barcelos, R. H., Dantas, D. C., & Sénécal, S. (February 2018). Watch Your Tone: How a Brand's Tone of Voice on Social Media Influences Consumer Responses. *Journal of Interactive Marketing, 41*, 60-80.

Breitsohl, J., Kunz, W., & Dowell, D. (2015).). Does the host match the content? A taxonomical update on online consumption communities. *Journal of Marketing Management, 31*(9-10), 1040-1064.

Brogan, C. (2010). *Social Media 101: Tactics and Tips to Develop Your Business Online.* Hoboken, NJ: Wiley.

Casaló, L., Flavián, C., & Guinalíu, M. (2007). The impact of participation in virtual brand communities on consumer trust and loyalty: The case of free software. *Online Information Review, 31*(6), 775-792.

Chu, S.-C., & Kim, Y. (2011). Determinants of consumer engagement in electronic word-of-mouth (eWOM) in social networking sites. *International Journal of Advertising, 30*(1), 47-75.

Coelho, P. S., Rita, P., & Santos, Z. (July 2018). On the relationship between consumer-brand identification, brand community, and brand loyalty. *Journal of Retailing and Consumer Services, 43*, 101-110.

Dolan, R., & Goodman, S. (December 2017). Succeeding on social media: Exploring communication strategies for wine marketing. *Journal of Hospitality and Tourism Management, 33*, 23-30.

Dwivedi, A. (May 2015). A higher-order model of consumer brand engagement and its impact on loyalty intentions. *Journal of Retailing and Consumer Services, 24*, 100-109.

Enginkaya, E., & Yilmaz, H. (25. August 2014). What drives consumers to interact with brands through social media? A motivation scale development study. *Procedia-Social and Behavioral Sciences, 148*, 219-226.

Erdogomus, I., & Cicek, M. (12. October 2012). The Impact of Social Media Marketing on Brand Loyalty. *Procedia - Social and Behavioral Sciences, 58*, 1353-1360.

Galati, A., Crescimanno, M., Tinervia, S., & Fagnani, F. (June 2017). Social media as a strategic marketing tool in the Sicilian wine industry: Evidence from Facebook. *Wine Economics and Policy, 6*(1), 40-47.

Habibi, M., Laroche, M., & Richard, M.-O. (August 2014). The roles of brand community and community engagement in building brand trust on social media. *Computers in Human Behavior, 37*, 152-161.

Hollebeek, L., Glynn, M., & Brodie, R. (May 2014). Consumer Brand Engagement in Social Media: Conceptualization, Scale Development and Validation. *Journal of Interactive Marketign, 28*(2), 149-165.

Kaplan, A., & Haenlein, M. (2010). Users of the world unite! The challenges and opportunities of Social Media. *Business horizons, 53*(1), 59-68.

Keller , K., Parameswaran, M., & Jacob, I. (2011). *Strategic Brand Management: Building, Measuring and Managing Equity.* Pearson Education India.

Laroche, M., Habibi, M. R., & Richard, M.-O. (2013). To bo or not to be in social media: How brand loyalty is affected by social media? *International Journal of Information Management, 33*(1), 76-82.

Leek, S., Canning, L., & Houghton, D. (April 2016). Revisiting the Task Media Fit Model in the era of Web 2.0: Twitter use and interaction in the healthcare sector. *Industrial Marketing Management, 54*, 25-32.

Makri, K., & Schlegelmilch, B. (November 2017). Time orientation and engagement with social networking sites: A cross-cultural study in Austria, China and Uruguay. *Journal of Business Research, 80*, 155-163.

Martin, S. (2017). Stakeholder dialogue on Facebook: Findings from German, Austrian and Swiss puplic utilities. *International Journal of Energy Sector Managemant, 11*(2), 257-267.

McAlexander, J., Schouten, J., & Koenig , H. (January 2002). Building Brand Community. *Journal of Marketing, 66*(1), 38-54.

Muntinga, D., Moorman, M., & Smit, E. (2011). Introducing COBRAs: Exploring motivations for brand-related social media use. *International Journal of Advertising, 30*(1), 13-46.

Nisar, T., & Whitehead, C. (September 2016). Brand interactions and social media: Enhancing user loyalty through social networking sites. *Computer in Human Behaviour, 62*, 743-753.

Osei-Frimpong, K., & McLean, G. (March 2018). Examining online social brand engagement: A social prescence theory perspective. *Technological Forecasting and Social Change, 128*, 10-21.

Saravanakumar, M., & SuganthaLakshmi, T. (2012). Social Media Marketing. *Life Science Journal, 9*(4), 4444-4451.

Schau, H. J., Muñiz, A. M., & Arnould, E. J. (September 2009). How Brand Community Practices Create Value. *Journal of Marketing, 73*(5), 30-51.

Simon, F., & Tossan, V. (April 2018). Does brand-consumer social sharing matter? A relational framework of customer engagement to brand-hosted social media. *Journal of Business Research, 85*, 175-184.

Statistics Austria. (18. 10 2017). *ICT Usage in Enterprises.* Von Statistics Austria: https://www.statistik.at/web_en/statistics/EnergyEnvironmentInnovationMob ility/information_society/ict_usage_in_enterprisese/114997.html abgerufen

Swani, K., Milne, G., Brown, B., George Assaf, A., & Donthu, N. (April 2017). What messages to post? Evaluating the popularity of social media communications in business versus consumer markets. *Industrial Marketing Management, 62*, 77-87.

Szolnoki, G., Taits, D., Hoffmann, C., Ludwig, R., Thach, L., Dolan , R., . . . Wilson, D. (June 2014). A cross-cultural comparison of social media usage in the wine business. *Proceedings of the 8th AWBR International Conference*, (p. 28-30).

Szolnoki, G., Taits, D., Nagel, M., & Fortunato, A. (2014). Using social media in the wine business: An exploratory study from Germany. *International Journal of Wine Research, 26*(2), 80-96.

Tajudeen, F., Jaafar, N., & Ainin, S. (April 2018). Understanding the impact of social media usage among organizations. *Information & Management, 55*(3), 308-321.

Verhoef, P., Reinartz, W., & Krafft, M. (2010). Customer Engagement as a New Perspective in Customer Management. *Journal of Service Research, 13*(3), 247-252.

Webster, J., & Watson, R. (2002). Analyzing the Past to Prepare for the Future: Writing a Literature Review. *MIS Quarterly, 26*(2), xiii-xxiii.

Yoshida, M., Gordon, B., Nakazawa, M., Shibuya, S., & Fujiwara, N. (2018). Bridging the gap between social media and behavioral brand loyalty. *Electronic Commerce Research and Applications, 28*, 2018-218.

ANNEX

Annex 1: Brief Literature Analysis

Author	Title	Year	Research Question	Methodology	Findings
Tahir M. Nisar, Caroline Whitehead	Brand interactions and social media: Enhancing user loyalty through social networking sites	2016	How user loyalty can be achieved and maintained through social networking sites?	Online survey with 530 participants (users of retail services). Survey participants were drawn from a representative panel of retail consumers operated by a global market research	Brands and consumer satisfaction are both positively related to users' behavioural loyalty. A level of trust is also established between the brand and consumers who follow brand pages on social media.
Sheena Leek, Louise Canning, David Houghton	Revisiting the Task Media Fit Model in the ear of Web 2.0: Twitter use and interaction in the healthcare sector	2016	Refinement of the Task Media Fit Model using business marketers' use of Twitter and followers' responses to tweeted messages	Preliminary & main investigative phases; Preliminary: identified suitable Twitter accounts; Main investigation: analysing the links and the engagement for the tweet	Business marketers use different embedded media according to the function of a tweet message. Followers responses to those messages do not vary with the task performed by the tweet, while the responses differ with the type of embedded link.
Masayuki Yoshida, Brian S. Gordon, Makoto Nakazawa, Shigeki Shibuya, Naoyuki Fujiwara	Bridging the gap between social media and behavioural brand loyalty	2018	What is the relationship between consumer responses in social networks and behavioural brand loyalty	Data collection from 309 panel registrants of an online research panel service	Online brand community identification has a positive influence on brand-related social media engagement.

Author	Title	Year	Research Question	Methodology	Findings
Pedro Simones Coelho; Paulo Rita, Zelia Raposo Santos	On the relationship between consumer-brand identification, brand community, and brand loyalty	2018	What is the role of consumer engagement on social media and its relationship with brand identity and consumer-brand identification?	Qualitative analysis (in-depth interviews) with experts and focus group discussions with consumers	Consumers engaged in social media brand communities may develop positive attitudes towards the brand (increasing trust, loyalty and consumer-brand identification)
G. Szolnoki, D. Taits, C. Hoffmann, R. Ludwig, Liz Thach, R. Dolan, S. Goodman, C. Habel, S. Forbes, N. Marinelli, D. Wilson, A. Mantonakis et al.	A cross-cultural comparison of social media usage in the wine business	2014	How is social media utilized in the different wine industries around the worls?	Questionnaire (translated into different languages) using online survey software; response rate was between 25 and 427 wineries	Social media has been accepted and is now widely used by wineries around the world as a communication tool. There is a significant difference between European and overseas countries
Antonino Galati, Maria Crescimanno, Salvatore Tinervia, Francesco Fagnani	Social media as a strategic marketing tool in the Sicilian wine industry: Evidence from Facebook	2017	What are a frim's social media efforts and what are the managerial characterisitics?	Data on 45 wineries was collected and analysed using a model that considers 3 different dimensions of the firms' activity on the social platform.	Especially small firms have become involved with social media.

Author	Title	Year	Research Question	Methodology	Findings
Rebecca Dolan, Steve Goodman	Succeeding on social media: Exploring communication strategies for wine marketing	2017	What is the communication like on social media from the perspective of the brand and the consumers?	Netnography and in-depth interviews of Australian wine brands active on social media	The 3 main communication orientation result in different responses amongst consumers, impacting brand recall, relationship building, brand personality perception, sense of community and product performance perception.
Irem Eren Erdogmus, Mesut Cicek	The impact of social media marketing on brand loyalty	2012	What is the effect of social media marketing on brand loyalty?	Structured questionnaire in Turkey of people who follow at least one brand on social media	Brand loyalty is positively affected if the brand offers advantageous campaigns, relevant content, popular contents or appears on various platforms and offers applications on social media.
Ebru Enginkaya, Hakan Yilmaz	What drives consumers to interact with brands through social media? A motivation scale development study.	2014	What drives consumers to interact with brands through social media?	Multi-item scale, statements in a 7-point response from 0-6.	The 5 distinct motivations are: brand affiliation, Investigation, opportunity seeking, conversation and Entertainment

Author	Title	Year	Research Question	Methodology	Findings
Françoise Simon, Vesselina Tossan	Does brand-consumer social sharing matter? A relational framework of consumer engagement to brand-hosted social media	2018	Does brand-consumer social sharing matter?	Sample of brands' Facebook page users; 4 dimensions: brand intimacy, brand individual recognition, brand influence and brand community belonging	Satisfaction and brand gratitude are media-driving variables; Gratitude is valued higher than satisfaction when it comes to engagement on social media
Kofi Osei-Frimpong, Graeme McLean	Examining online social brand engagement: A social presence theory perspective	2018	What is the influence of social presence on social brand engagement and the effects on firm-generated content and consumer commitment.	Quantitative survey with 738 consumers with prior experience in following or engaging with brands on social media, randomly interviewed using an online questionnaire	Social brand engagement encourages consumers to increase their intention to use the brand and also engage in electronic word of mouth.
Gergely Szolnoki, Taits Dimitri, Moritz Nagel, Alessio Forunato	Using social media in the wine business: An exploratory study from Germany	2014	Which social media tools are used by German wineries/in the German wine industry	Study with 321 German wineries, online survey with customers of the wineries	60% of German wineries communicate with customers on social media; most used is Facebook

YOUR KNOWLEDGE HAS VALUE

www.ingramcontent.com/pod-product-compliance
Lightning Source LLC
LaVergne TN
LVHW042309060326
832902LV00009B/1372